SHUT UP
AND STAY MARRIED

THE SECRET TO MARRIAGE SUCCESS

YISROEL ROLL

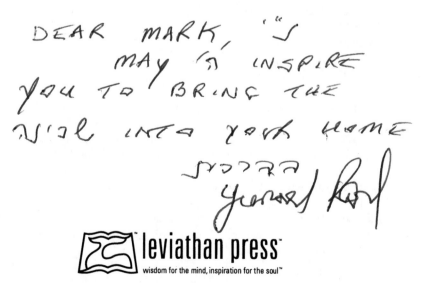

DEAR MARK, "ש
MAY ש INSPIRE
YOU TO BRING THE
שלום INTO YOUR HOME

בברכה
Yisroel Roll

leviathan press
wisdom for the mind, inspiration for the soul™

Shut Up and Stay Married
The Secret to Marriage Success
by Yisroel Roll

Published by
Leviathan Press
2505 Summerson Road
Baltimore, Maryland 21209
443-939-0828
leviathanpress@gmail.com

ISBN 978-1-881927-02-0

First printing: February 2011

Layout & cover design   Block Design / blockdesign@gmail.com
Editorial services   Sharon Goldinger / PeopleSpeak

Available to the trade by Ingram

All books from Leviathan Press are available at bulk order discounts for educational, promotional and fund raising purposes. For information leviathanpress@gmail.com.

For Julie

TABLE OF CONTENTS

FOREWARD

Dr. Abraham J. Twerski

My dear friend, Yisroel Roll, has written an excellent book that will help preserve many marriages; but some people may be scared off by the title *Shut-up and Stay Married*. They may think that he is advocating the limiting of communication between husband and wife. Nothing of the sort!

There is a commonly heard adage, "Sticks and stones can break your bones but words won't hurt you any." I can't think of anything that can possibly be as false. To the contrary, as painful as physical wounds may be to endure, they do heal. The harm done by unkind words may be much slower to heal, if ever.

If we stay in the sun too long and sustain severe sunburn, our skin becomes so sensitive that even a soft touch may cause pain. We all have our days when we are extremely irritable, and our emotions are "sunburned" so that we may feel severe pain even with minor provocation. The pain may be magnified many times by an unkind, inconsiderate or insulting comment.

It is with regard to such comments that Yisroel Roll cautions spouses to "shut-up and stay married."

Dorothy Nevill said, "The real art of conversation is not only to say the right thing in the right place, but to leave unsaid the wrong thing at the tempting moment."

A word is like an arrow, which once it leaves the bow, cannot be recalled. Once you have uttered a word that offends someone, you cannot recall it. Even profuse apologies may not be able to erase its effects.

If one can "shut-up" for even a few moments when one feels like saying something in anger or frustration, these few moments of silence give the person the opportunity to think how to say something that will convey a positive message without a sting.

And what then, of positive communication? Think of how many relationships are shattered because of some people's inability or hesitance to express love and gratitude, or to admit one's mistakes. How many broken homes could have been preserved if the three magic phrases—I love you, I thank you, and I was wrong—would have been voiced more frequently. Whether between husband and wife, or between friends, these three simple phrases can bind and reinforce a relationship.

The resistance to expressing love, gratitude and remorse are in large part due to a lack of self esteem. A person plagued by feelings of inferiority and unworthiness may feel incapable of being loved, hence he cannot love another. He may feel that being thankful to another person for a favor received constitutes indebtedness, and he does not wish to feel obligated or beholden to others. Finally, a person with low self esteem may be threatened by the recognition, let alone the admission, that he was wrong.

Listen to the simple strategies set out by Yisroel Roll in *Shut Up and Stay Married.* He provides us with a much needed prescription for the healing of feelings of unworthiness and inadequacy which will restore you to resilience and self worth- and revive your feelings of love and your marriage.

—Abraham J. Twerski, MD

Dr. Abraham Twerski, MD is the founder and medical director of the Gateway Rehabilitation Center in Aliquippa, Pennsylvania and has played a vital role in the recovery of more than 40,000 patients. A psychiatrist, and chemical dependency counselor, New York magazine calls him a "near mythic figure" among his patients and followers. He served as the Chief of Psychiatry at Pittsburgh's St. Francis General hospital from 1965-1985 and was Clinical Professor of Psychiatry at Pittsburgh School of Medicine. He has authored 65 books on self-esteem development, spirituality and contemporary thought.

ACKNOWLEDGMENTS

I am grateful to the following people who have contributed to the development of this book:

Jonathan Symons, of London, England, for his friendship and support.

Gary Davis, of Greenwich, Connecticut, for his advice and support.

Gary Torgow, of Detroit, Michigan, for his guidance and encouragement.

Sharon Goldinger, of Laguna Hills, California, for her expert editing of the manuscript.

Rachel Block, of Houston, Texas, for her creative work on the book cover.

Sol Ehrentreu, of blessed memory, for his life-long friendship.

My wife, Julie, for believing in me.

Our children, for inspiring me.

INTRODUCTION

"**D**inner is hardly ever ready on time, and as a couple we never get anywhere on time. Why can't anything run on time around here? What kind of responsibility are the kids learning in our home if my wife can't get her act together?"

"My husband is always on the computer. The house could be on fire, and he wouldn't know it. When I sit down to talk to him, he keeps typing. Am I not at least as important as the computer? No wonder the kids don't respect me. My husband doesn't show me respect, so why should they?"

"The desk in the study has bills on it, the dining room table has bills on it, the kitchen table has bills on it, and no matter how many times I ask my wife to keep all the bills in one place, she spreads them out all over the house. The whole house is her office. And then she complains that the house is not organized."

Do these scenarios sound familiar? In each of them, a spouse is frustrated, thinking, "Why can't my spouse just act like a normal human being?" or, "Why can't he just give me some attention and love?" or, "Why can't she just show me some respect?"

When you are deeply hurt, you feel compelled to say something. You need to set the record straight. You need to make a comment so that your spouse's behavior won't get out of hand. But when you do say something, your spouse comes back with a complaint to counter yours, and that hurts. Then you don't talk for two days at least, and the argument takes on a life of its own and escalates. You wonder, "Why can't I have some peace and quiet? Why is there so much tension in our house?"

This book offers hands-on strategies to create a peaceful marriage.

- You will learn to how get along without hurting each other.
- You will learn how to just "let things go" and not comment on them.
- You will learn how to live and let live.
- You will learn how to bring back the positive feelings you had for your spouse when you were first in love.

This book will give you amazing insight into family dynamics and you will learn how to shut up and stay married!

The book is divided into three parts. Part 1 is called "How to Achieve Emotional Independence." It discusses a unique approach to marriage and it is the key to the book. Usually, self-help books on marriage focus on what you can do for your spouse and how you can be there for your spouse. This book starts with you. Before you can relate to your spouse, you have to learn how to relate to yourself. You will learn how to discover your strengths and nurture yourself. Then you will learn how to gain emotional independence by being in tune with your emotions and by becoming the master of them. After you integrate these lessons, nothing your spouse does or says will be able to set you off. Your spouse's comments or behavior may still push your buttons, but you will learn to hold your response, shut up and be happy about it.

Part 2 is called "How to Create a Good Marriage". Once you have learned the techniques in part 1 by becoming free of instinctive and impulsive reactions, then you will learn how to use your strengths to build a positive and loving relationship with your spouse. Good communication is an art which can be learned. In this section you will learn how to motivate yourself with a positive mindset, an attitude of gratitude and active listening. You will learn the techniques of personal mind control and how to inspire yourself. Here too, you will learn that the key to a good marriage lies in your own hands—it's all about you—not your spouse.

Part 3 is called "How to Create a Happy Family," and is about becoming a successful parent. Marriage is impacted greatly by children, and much of marriage is learning how to work together with your spouse to successfully raise children. In this part you will learn innovative strategies to motivate children to do the right thing. Again, it's not about getting the children to behave, rather, it's about your attitude to parenting, consistency, motivation and parenting strategies.

In order to use the strategies in this book successfully you will first learn to put yourself onto the same page as your spouse. (That's why you should read the book together with your spouse.) In each part of the book, you will find hands-on exercises that you will need to practice. Getting good at marriage is a joint effort, so read one chapter of the book, ask your spouse to read the same chapter, and then discuss the chapter's topic and try the exercises, together.

The names of people in the book are fictitious, but every event and scenario discussed in the book happened and is true. To avoid the awkwardness of "his or her," the pronouns for unnamed spouses generally have been alternated from example to example;

that is, one example refers to "her" and the next example refers to "his."

So this is a "his and hers" book. It's for both of you--which reminds me of a story.

Andrea and Sean had been married for two years and were like two ships passing in the night. Each felt that the other was selfish. After the infatuation had worn off, they realized that they shared little in common. One day, Steve, a mutual friend from out of town, called them and asked for some help. He was in serious trouble. Andrea and Sean each worked out separate plans to help their friend. As usual, they did not work together. Each came up with an idea to help. The next day, each drove four hours, in separate cars, to Steve's house to see what he or she could do to help. They arrived within an hour of each other.

Andrea and Sean sat down with Steve and gave him their ideas and their emotional support. The two worked the entire day on a plan to help their friend. To their amazement, they worked well together and realized that they actually shared the same values. At home that night they stayed up late talking about values and the aspirations and dreams they once shared and decided to give their marriage a real try. Shared values put them back on the same page and brought them back to working on their marriage. "His and hers" ideas to help Steve became their shared connection.

The goal of this book is to get you and your spouse back on the same page through using techniques and strategies that have worked for thousands of people. If you learn the secret of how to shut up, you will stay married, happily.

HOW TO ACHIEVE EMOTIONAL INDEPENDENCE

PART 1

CHAPTER 1   # SHUT UP

and Develop Trust

Rick and Lisa had been married for thirteen years and were desperate to have children. They tried everything, including relaxing vacations and "not thinking about it." Still, nothing. They went to see a spiritual guru overseas, and when they walked into his room, the guru said to them, "I know why you are here and I cannot give you a blessing to have children. You do not have a good marriage. You constantly criticize each other and do not accept each other. I will not bless you to bring children into a home without peace."

Rick was devastated. Lisa, with her feminine intuition, already knew that the reason they were not having children was their lack of mutual respect. As they walked out of the guru's home, Rick made a silent vow: "I will never criticize my wife again." And he kept his promise. Twelve months later Lisa gave birth to twins. Since then they have had two more children. Rick and Lisa are happy, and their children are thriving.

Rick and Lisa discovered the secret to marriage success: shut up and stay married. If spouses are able to control their tongues and refrain from criticizing or complaining about their spouse's behavior, then the negativity and resentment will be removed, and the relationship will have room to breathe. The marriage partners will go back to being accepted and accepting of each other. Then the feelings of positivity will return. The spouses will give each other space, and the natural respect they have for each other will return.

Notice that I haven't used the word "love." That word is too theoretical. Love is just a concept, an idea. But we cannot live our lives based on abstract concepts or ideas. We need to live practical everyday lives. So we need to create a user-friendly, practical definition of and approach to love.

Love means trust. You trust that your spouse will not hurt your feelings.

That is the key. When you criticize your spouse, you cause a breach of trust because the criticism or complaint hurts her feelings. When you criticize, you convey that your spouse is not measuring up to your expectations, that your spouse is letting you and the relationship down. That criticism destroys the peace of the home because your spouse cannot feel emotionally safe in her own home. Criticism and negativity erodes the trust we hope for in marriage, and then love simply has no chance to take root.

You might say to me, "Am I supposed to sit there and take it? Just watch him mess up our lives?" Precisely. The antidote to divorce is to keep quiet, say nothing, hold your tongue, and bite your lip. In other words, shut up and stay married. Why?

The reason people get married is not to find happiness. They marry to find acceptance and validation. Yes, the workplace, our peer relationships, and our family bonds can be tough to manage, and the intimate relationship of husband and wife is where we should be able to find emotional safety and security. In the marriage relationship, we should be able to be ourselves without being told we are not good enough.

Think about it: where else are you supposed to find some peace in this world if not within your own home, a safe haven from the turmoil of life?

So the key to a successful marriage is building trust. This requires both parties to accept each other as they are and refrain from criticism and put-downs. In other words, stay married by exhibiting self-control and not criticizing. Granted, that takes amazing self-restraint and inner strength. And since only half of us have found that strength, the United States has a 50 percent divorce rate. Those who have managed to stay married have developed the art of self-control. They have learned how to shut up and stay married. Now, let us learn to develop that self-control.

CHAPTER 2

SHUT UP
and Share Your Feelings

You may be thinking, "Do you mean to tell me that I can't complain to my spouse?"

No, you can complain to your spouse about your boss, your mother, your children, and your bad hair day—but you can't complain to your spouse about your spouse. You cannot make comments like the following—even if they are true:

- You are embarrassing.
- You are lazy.
- You are inconsiderate.
- You are being unfair.
- You are fat.
- You are letting yourself go.
- You are not a good provider.

"What!" you might think. I cannot be honest with my spouse? I thought trust was based on honesty!"

Yes, you can be honest about your feelings—but not at the expense of the feelings of your spouse.

So what you can say is this:

- I am feeling frustrated.
- I am feeling hurt.
- I feel embarrassed.
- I am disappointed.
- I am feeling lonely.
- I am feeling unloved.

These are called "I" messages because you can express how you feel using the word "I." Messages like the ones in the first list use "you" instead of "I." "You" messages put your partner on the defensive and undermine trust.

A "you" message points a finger at your spouse and makes the relationship unsafe and insecure. When you use "I" messages, on the other hand, you keep your relationship in the "acceptance mode." You are validating that your spouse is okay just the way he is while expressing that you are uncomfortable with a situation. When your spouse hears that you are feeling upset, he is more likely to ask how he can help you, than when you accuse him of being the cause of the problem.

Success in marriage requires using a two step process: 1. Refrain from criticizing your spouse and, 2. Create a positive atmosphere in the home through praise and encouragement (as we will discuss in part 2). Then, when you are upset about a situation having to do with your spouse and you use an "I" message, the trust in the relationship will be maintained. Doing so, will allow your spouse to identify with your pain, feel empathy, and help you resolve the issue. This is true even if your spouse contributed to your feeling hurt, embarrassed, or unloved. Why? Because you have already established and are now maintaining an ongoing relationship of trust by not criticizing your spouse and each spouse can then "take the heat" if the feeling is expressed in the form of an "I" message.

The "I" message format allows your spouse to feel safe and secure in your presence. Your spouse knows that you will not take pot shots at him and will not use those "dig" comments that undermine the emotional safety of the relationship.

This system requires a shift in attitude toward marriage. Obviously, with the divorce rate at 50 percent, something is going wrong. We have been too free with our language, and we have failed to be sensitive to the feelings of our spouses. Our attitude has been: "let it all hang out," and we have said whatever is on our minds, even if it is hurtful.

We have also gone wrong by misusing the terms "husband" and "wife." They are too impersonal. These terms make it sound like spouses are playing a role. They depersonalize a partner's sense of self and individuality. Your spouse is more than your husband or your wife. Your spouse is a person with feelings. You have to appreciate his or her vulnerability and treat him or her in private as if you were both in public. In public you would hardly be insensitive or critical of your spouse. That should be the rule in the privacy of your own home as well.

CHAPTER 3 # SHUT UP
and Stop Criticizing

Asking you to not criticize your spouse is asking you to rise to a seemingly superhuman level of self-control. That's because so many of our spouse's faults bother us:

- The way she holds a fork
- The way he sleeps
- The way she is always fifteen minutes late for everything
- The way he always cooks the chicken the same old way
- The way she speaks to her mother on the phone
- The way he keeps the house
- The way she works all the time and never has time for me
- The way he never cleans up the den
- The way she never exercises

We, as spouses, enjoy commenting on these flaws, and we feel justified in doing so. Often we may feel that we have solid evidence that our spouse is wrong, or we may have had our opinions about our spouse's behavior confirmed by family, friends, or therapists. However, marriage is not about being right or wrong—that attitude belongs in the courtroom or in a research paper. In marriage what counts is trust, which is the basis of love.

The competitive spirit is not conducive to marriage harmony. Spouses keeping score undermines the trust and safety of the relationship. Competition is for business or the sports field. But in marriage you need to develop a secure working relationship so that even if your spouse is wrong about something, you control yourself and refrain from commenting or demeaning him.

You may say, "I have to correct my spouse, otherwise she will not grow. My job is to help my spouse develop, and if I don't comment on what she is doing wrong she will never know what areas she has to change." But you are not your spouse's mother, father, teacher, judge, or probation officer. These roles put spouses into adversarial conflict. Correcting your spouse does not engender safety or security; instead, it puts your spouse on the defensive. Assuming a parenting role toward your spouse does not breed trust. It actually breeds mistrust.

To understand why you should not say something to stop your spouse's behavior, let's talk about correcting or disciplining children for a moment.

Have you ever noticed that no matter how many times you tell your children to do their homework, clean up their room, or stop whining, they still don't listen, and that even if you give them "consequences" (instead of the old-fashioned punishments) nothing seems to work? That's because, as psychological studies have shown, you cannot change someone's behavior through criticism, rebuke, discipline, lecture, or argument. You can only get someone to change through positive reinforcement of positive behavior. For example, when you praise your children or give them tickets or prizes for consistently cleaning up their room, doing their homework, or treating their sister nicely, you will get more of that positive behavior. In psychology this system is called "operant conditioning." According to educational psychologists this principle applies in learning as well. The way to stop negative behavior is by ignoring the negatives and praising the positives. This technique is called "extinguishing" the negative behavior.

Now back to spouses. You will not get your spouse to change through nagging, complaining, pot-shots, or digs. Not only will this approach fail, it also will actually breed resentment, which will undermine trust. The only way to get a spouse to do what you want is through positive reinforcement of positive behavior.

You might be thinking, "I don't care if positive reinforcement will work. I just want to get back at my spouse for hurting me."

The reason trying to get back at your spouse is a bad idea is that it will lead to an escalation of negativity. If you feel that you and your spouse are locked into a cycle of negativity, then you need to break the cycle by seeking counseling or follow the "I" message system discussed in chapter 2.

You might be thinking, "That's not fair. My spouse is the one who is always wrong!" But someone has to break this cycle, and it might as well be you.

Remember, the spouses in successful marriage are not focused on winning a battle or being right or wrong. They focus on building a foundation of mutual trust. Trust has nothing to do with being right or wrong. It has everything to do with building a safe haven in your home where love can enter.

CHAPTER 4 # SHUT UP

and Feel Good About Yourself

Y ou may be thinking, "Successful marriage sounds so simple. Just refrain from criticizing my spouse— I could have figured that out myself!"

But shutting up is not so simple, is it? If it were, we would not have a 50 percent divorce rate for first marriages, and those marriages that <u>are</u> still together would be a lot happier. So what is the key to holding your tongue? How can you achieve this superhuman feat of not digging at your spouse? How can you let the issue go?

The answer is cultivating self esteem. Your own. If you feel good about yourself, then you don't feel the need to say anything when your spouse does something you do not approve of. However, let's be clear. This idea does not apply to spouses' behaviors that are emotionally, physically, or sexually abusive. Those behaviors are not acceptable, and they must be stopped immediately. Involve counselors, professionals, or the police if abuse happens or is happening. Do not be silent.

In non abusive situations, most of the arguments and issues with your spouse probably started with a seemingly innocuous action or comment. Your spouse said something that struck you the wrong way, did something that wasn't exactly the way you liked it, or made that annoying gesture that you just can't stand. On these issues you can express your feelings through the "I" messages technique we discussed in chapter 2. However, in cases of sexual, physical or emotional abuse by your spouse, "I messages" will not stop the problem.

But when these types of abuse are not in evidence, yet friction, negativity, criticism, and a lack of trust exist in the relationship, then the source of the problem may very well be the low self-esteem of the spouse who is negative or critical or the low self-esteem of the spouse who is suffering from this negativity and criticism.

Low self-esteem can develop in many ways. It develops in children when parents, who themselves have low self-esteem, use power, control, and criticism to discipline. Teachers (and bullies) who use this heavy-handed critical style also have low self-esteem. A constant barrage of negativity from parents, teachers, or peers can lead a child to develop an impression in his subconscious mind that he is inadequate and unworthy of love. The child thinks, "Why are those around me so critical of me? I must be bad!" And this low self-esteem becomes a mind-set that the child carries into adulthood. The feeling of unworthiness and inadequacy becomes the child's worldview.

Why do children form this impression of themselves as being inadequate? Children have no sense of "self." They do not have the reflective or introspective capacity to evaluate their unique personalities. They lack self-awareness. The only way children learn about themselves is through interactions, feedback, and appraisals from their parents, teachers, and peers. When a child hears, "Don't touch that," "Don't spill that," "Don't do that," Bad boy," "Bad girl," a few times a day for ten years, she will integrate a sense of "badness" into her psyche.

Another source of low self-esteem in children is the divorce of parents. And with such a high divorce rate, the large number of children who feel insecure is no surprise. By and large, most children need two loving parents to feel secure and protected. When parents divorce, children subconsciously blame themselves for the divorce, in many cases. A child may think, "If I was a better boy, my parents wouldn't have argued so much." These feelings of guilt and self-blame are evident even when the children become adults and surface as depression or low self-esteem. I have treated many adult clients who blame themselves for their parents' divorce, sometimes twenty five years later.

Whatever the cause of their low self-esteem, when these children grow up and get married, they carry within them feelings of inadequacy. This is called the "unfinished business" of their childhood. As a result, one negative comment by a spouse triggers their underlying low self-esteem, and they respond in anger, pain, and hurt. If the spouse felt good about himself, then he would use an "I" message and say, "I feel hurt." He would not respond, "Well, look who's talking" or "You don't speak nicely to my parents." When spouses respond in this fashion, the negativity escalates into a full-blown argument that has little to do with the original hurtful comment.

This negativity works both ways. The spouse who consistently utters negative comments may also be suffering from low self-esteem. Critical people may be covering up their own bad feelings about themselves by projecting those faults onto their spouses. In other words, if you don't like your spouse's behavior in a certain area, you probably do the same action in a different form. You loathe the behavior so much in yourself that you see it in your spouse. As the saying goes: "If you criticize another, you reveal yourself."

How do you break out of this low self-esteem spiral that leads to constant criticism and recriminations? The next chapter will reveal the secret of how to liberate yourself from this unhealthy mode of being. The tools I discuss will change your life.

CHAPTER 5 # SHUT UP

and Repair Your
Low Self-Esteem

I f you want to stay married, you are going to need healthy self-esteem. The techniques in this chapter will help you change your negative self-image into a healthy one, or maybe they will be a way to gain your sense of "self" for the first time.

Below is a Wheel of Strengths. Each of the six sections of the Wheel represents a different area of your self-concept: Intellect, Social Skills, Character, Spirituality, Family, and Physicality.[1] These six sections of the wheel represent aspects of your personality that lead to your forming an overall self image.

You relate to the world from the perspective of your intellect, social skills, character strengths, spiritual leanings, family background, and physical attributes. In each of these areas you "esteem" or measure your intellect, your people skills, your values, yourself as a family person, your spirituality, and your body image. Each of these areas, by themselves, is a mini world for you. When taken together they lead to an overall picture of your "self."

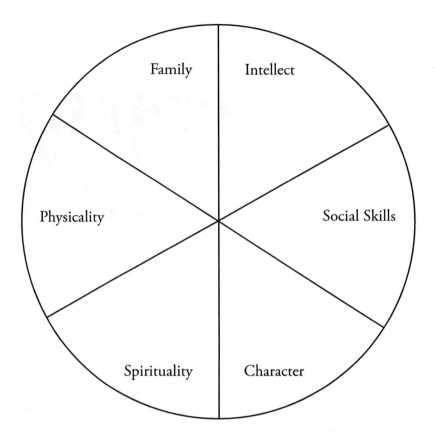

In each area of the Wheel, please write down two or three of your strengths or personal abilities.

The following questions will help you identify the types of strengths that you can include in each of the sections of your Wheel of Strengths so that you can discover more about the personal power that you bring to your marriage.

- Intellect: Are you street-smart? Do you have common sense? Are you book smart/academic? Are you quick witted? Do you have a sense of humor? Are you a problem solver? Articulate? Bright? Intellectual? Organized?

- <u>Social Skills</u>: Are you a good friend? Do you have a close friend? Are you a good listener? Can you keep a secret? Are you helpful to those in need? Are you involved in the community? Are you dependable? Do you encourage others? Do you build people up when they are down? Are you reassuring? Loyal? Committed? Loving? Sharing? Tolerant? Understanding? Would you help a friend change a flat tire at three in the morning in the rain?

- <u>Character</u>: Which of these character traits best describe your strengths: affectionate, compassionate, considerate, appreciative, gracious, giving, patient, truthful, honest, creative, forgiving, calm, gutsy, disciplined, persistent, positive, resilient, sensitive, spontaneous, visionary, ambitious, driven? Add your own traits to this list.

- <u>Spirituality</u>: Do you reflect on the meaning of life or on how to improve yourself? Do you enjoy the majesty of nature? Do you make moral choices? Do you forgive others? Do you enjoy doing acts of kindness for others? Do you sacrifice your desires for others?

- <u>Family</u>: Are you a respected member of your family? Do you respect your spouse and children? Do you encourage your family? Does your family encourage you? Do you encourage independent thinking in your family? Do you make a positive contribution to the well-being of your family? Are you loved? Do you give love?

- <u>Physicality</u>: Do you work out? Do you eat healthy? Do you contribute to the efficiency of your home? Do you like your body? Do you play any sports? Do you do outdoor activities?

Now that you have surveyed your life strengths, you have probably noticed that these six sections are actually six pathways you use to relate to and interact with the world. These areas, when taken together, comprise your overall "identity." Your identity or "self" is, in essence, your destiny. These character resources combine to create your uniqueness. Your intellectual self-concept, social self-concept, character self-concept, spiritual self-concept, family self-concept, and physical self-concept are unique in the world. Never has there been another person with your particular set of strengths—and there never will be. You are here in this world to use your strengths to make a positive contribution to society.

As you take an inventory of your strengths, you can begin to develop the attitude that you are a valued, worthy, and talented player in the opportunity called life. You can use your strengths to work toward your goals. If you see yourself as a valuable person, then you can begin to see yourself as a valued marriage partner. But before you focus on being a friend to your marriage partner, you have to become friends with yourself. If you appreciate your own value, you acquire the key ingredient to have a happy marriage—a positive self-image. Then you can begin to believe in your own ability to succeed in your relationship with your spouse.

Now, if your spouse says something hurtful or does something you do not approve of, before reacting, take out your Wheel of Strengths and study it. You are okay. You are fine just the way you are. The fact that your spouse doesn't see your strengths at this moment does not matter. Maybe she is having a bad day. But you are always having a good day because you have an awareness of your intrinsic value—just look at, integrate, and appreciate the strengths on your Wheel. The Wheel of Strengths is the basis for your self-esteem. If you recognize the values and abilities on your Wheel, you can begin to esteem and like your "self'."

The definition of healthy self-esteem has two parts: (1) you have intrinsic value and worth and are therefore worthy of love and acceptance, and (2) you have the talents and resources to meet life's challenges.

Both parts of the definition find their expression on your Wheel of Strengths. On the Wheel you will find your character values as well as your abilities. Use your Wheel as a daily resource. Make four photocopies of it and put one on your fridge, one in your car, one on your desk, and one on your night table. Learn it, study it, and integrate it into your psyche. Add to it. Every time you experience a special event and you survive it, add that newly discovered strength to your Wheel. Show the Wheel to your spouse and ask him to help you add to it. Draw a Wheel for your spouse and help him complete it. Discuss and express to your spouse how you appreciate his strengths. When you become aware of your Wheel of Strengths and the Wheel of Strengths of your spouse you will create an emotional bond with each other that you both feel, and value. You will start to see each other's unique qualities and put your foibles and faults into perspective.

Recognizing your faults is a sign of humility, but recognizing your strengths is not a sign of conceit. When you recognize your strengths and you use them to serve others and make a difference in the world, you are not being haughty. You are actually performing an act of humility. How so?

Whenever I present a self-esteem workshop, I ask the participants to record their strengths in various categories outlined in the Wheel of Strengths. Invariably, one or two of the participants sit staring at the Wheel as if they are at a loss. They can't seem to find anything positive to write about themselves.

"Perfect," I say to myself. "Working through that struggle is the reason they have come to the workshop. They have low self-esteem, and I hope I can help them." When I ask them if they need help, one will invariably say, "I can't write down my strengths because it would be a sign of conceit and haughtiness to write down all these positive attributes. I just can't bring myself to do it."

To become aware of your personal strengths and positive attributes does not amount to conceit or haughtiness. You show conceit when you speak about and revel in your past accomplishments, name dropping and bragging about awards you have received. To record your strengths, however, is actually a display of modesty and humility because you are taking an inventory of your attributes in order to figure out how you can continue to serve others with those strengths in the future. Conceit is past oriented, whereas humility is future oriented.

Becoming aware of character values like compassion, creativity, or empathy is humbling because once you identify them, then you become responsible for using them in your dealings with others. The recognition of your inner abilities and talents makes you realize that they have been given to you in order to help you actualize and maximize your potential—and you can begin by using them in your relationship with your spouse.

Here is some homework. Buy yourself a small journal or notebook and at the end of the day take out your Wheel of Strengths. Look at the Wheel and review your day in your mind. Make a list of the six categories of the Wheel and record how you used or actualized the strengths of your personality today. For example, if you initiated a word of kindness toward your spouse then write that down next to Character. If you listened to your spouse and were emotionally supportive write down "Empathy to Spouse" next to Social Skills. If you organized a play-date for your child write down "social engineering" next to Intellect. Do this journaling every day for a month. You will become more aware of your personality strengths and will be more conscious of using them. This will build your sense of self and motivate you to be there for your spouse and children.

CHAPTER 6   # SHUT UP

and Discover
Your True Self

The key to discovering your true self lies in the Character section of the Wheel of Strengths. In this chapter you will discover what makes you uniquely "you." Identifying your values intellectually is not enough. You need to *experience* who you are. If you live your values you will be able to hold yourself back from saying something to your spouse that you would regret. In other words, if you discover your true self, you will be able to shut up and stay married.

You can experience your true self—otherwise known as your highest self or your soul self—by becoming aware of that part of you that is most spiritual, the part of you that acts most human and least animal. Animals don't have self-awareness, try to improve their behavior, learn from past mistakes, or think about the meaning of their lives. They can't overcome their instincts and make moral choices; they don't think about the future, empathize, aspire to a life of purpose, or forgive. Human beings do. When you think in this fashion or perform any of these actions, you are being spiritual.

Whenever you experience a surge of meaning within your being, whenever you feel that there is something more to life than what you see, you are tapping into an awareness of your spiritual self—your soul. For example, when you feel the sunset speaking to you, the soul within you is being activated. If you feel the mountain air give you renewed energy as you hike atop a mountain ridge, you are experiencing a connection to something bigger than yourself. You are feeling an awareness of your true self.

The awareness and appreciation of your soul self leads to a holistic sense of inner tranquility. This is your "soul state," a state of equilibrium and inner contentment. You feel aligned and one with the universe. The reason for this feeling goes deeper than just the beautiful scene that is inspiring you. You feel aligned and whole because you are one with your inner self, which is driven by your highest and best character trait. In this state of being, you feel a sense of wholeness and serenity. Everything in your life becomes clarified, and you feel that you can achieve anything.

You can put yourself into your soul state by *experiencing* your finest attribute. Begin by imagining a beautiful landscape or place that you find relaxing and rejuvenating. It may be the Grand Canyon, Niagara Falls, the Swiss Alps, the beach, an orchard, or a sunset. Go to that place in your mind, and describe the landscape to yourself with all its colors, sounds, and scents. Feel the place. Experience the sense of calm, relaxation, freedom, and expansiveness that you feel while in this place. You experience feelings of liberation, inspiration, and fulfillment in this place of external beauty because it reflects the Grand Canyon, Niagara Falls, the Alps, the beach, or the sunset that resides within you.

Your highest and best attribute is the essence of who you are. When you live by this attribute, you become aligned with the flow of the universe. You become one with the universe. You enter a state of inner serenity where nothing bothers you.

To discover your highest attribute, review the following list of character traits and identify the one that drives and motivates you the most. In other words, which attribute exemplifies the theme of your life?

- Consistency
- Perseverance
- Power
- Leadership
- Compassion
- Empathy
- Graciousness
- Sincerity
- Patience
- Loving-kindness
- Truth
- Honesty
- Integrity
- Creativity
- Forgiving nature

When you recognize and activate your best attribute, you become truly alive, and you feel serenity and inner peace. When you are in this state of being, nothing can throw you off track because you are connected with truth. Self knowledge means connection to truth and to your true self. You don't believe an idea to be true—you know it is true.

In this state of being, self-doubt and anxious thoughts are irrelevant. Thoughts are merely electrical impulses from the brain. They are not "real" in the same way that the true self is real. Positive thoughts lead to good feelings, an elevated mood, and positive sensations in your body. Anxious thoughts lead to tense feelings, a depressed mood, and stress in your body. Thoughts fluctuate and cause our moods to fluctuate. Thoughts are part of the world of emotional fantasy. They are not objectively real.

The way to avoid the mood swings brought on by fluctuating thoughts is to leave your head space—leave your thoughts—and go to your soul state. Here, no thoughts of jealousy, hurt, frustration, or emotional angst are relevant, because you are connected to truth itself—to your true self.

Now let's try an experiment. Put yourself into your soul state by going to the Grand Canyon, Niagara Falls or Swiss Alps in your mind. Reflect and live in your true self, which really is your highest attribute. Now imagine your spouse saying he is upset with you. What happens to your mood? Nothing. Stay with serenity. Stay with wholeness. Stay in your soul state. You might have to concentrate harder on your highest attribute to stay in this mode.

Imagine your spouse doing something that annoys you. Stay in the soul state. What happens to your mood? Nothing. Would you take a pot-shot at your spouse while in this state? Not likely. You like this soul state because you are one with your true self, and no comment or behavior by your spouse can disturb your inner equilibrium. You are in such a state of oneness that nothing can affect you. When you learn to get good at accessing the soul state, you will have mastered emotional independence. Now you have learned the secret. You can now shut up and stay married.

It is one thing to get into your soul state and be so okay with yourself that you are able to shut up. It is quite another thing to get good at achieving this state. Self mastery takes practice. You need to find some quiet time for three minutes a day and practice going to your soul state, especially when nothing is bothering you. Get good at going to this inner serenity state so that when you are challenged by a comment or behavior by your spouse you can access your soul state in five seconds and then hold your tongue. When you can do this, that unnecessary argument will simply not happen.

CHAPTER 7

and Stop Escalating

It turns out then that the reason we are usually unable to shut up has nothing to do with our spouses and everything to do with ourselves. When we are uncomfortable and unhappy with ourselves, we lash out at the most convenient and available target—our spouses. The truth is that if we started to like ourselves, then the comments and behaviors of our spouses would not bother us, and we would not feel compelled to say anything to correct our spouses or set the record straight. Why? Because the record would already be straight—within our own selves.

What happens when our serenity or soul state is challenged? We feel like we have to respond. We need to defend ourselves. Our dignity has been challenged, and we need to stand up for ourselves. If we don't then we will be turned into a *shmatta* (Yiddish for "doormat").

The following technique will help you maintain your soul state and hold your tongue. Imagine yourself on a beach enjoying the expanse of water, the waves, and the setting sun as its orange rays flicker gently over the water. Just as you begin to luxuriate in this paradise, you look out over the horizon and see a giant oil tanker. It blocks out your view of the glorious sunset and darkens the sky. What do you do? You are so upset about this intrusion that you get into your rowboat, row out to the oil tanker, and climb aboard. You clamber over the deck and start opening the hatches. You begin shouting, "What are you doing blocking out my view of the sunset? Who owns this ship? What chutzpah you have to spoil my view!" In short, you are angry and you want that ship out of there!

The open view of the sunset represents your soul state. Everything is beautiful and idyllic. You are one with the world, and the glorious sunset inspires you and makes you feel whole. The oil tanker symbolizes a negative comment or behavior by your spouse. It blocks your view and upsets your equilibrium. So what do you do? You row out to the tanker that is bothering you to correct the situation. This action represents your negative response to your spouse. You defend yourself, saying, "Get out of my space!" The owner of the oil tanker—your spouse— responds by saying, "You don't own the ocean. I have just as much right to be here as you do." You get into an escalating argument with your oil-tanker spouse. And you both lose.

How do you solve the problem of an oil tanker blocking your sunset? The answer lies in what happens to oil tankers as they cross the horizon. That's right—they cross the horizon. The process takes a little time, but the tankers do eventually sail on and out of view. So too do irritating comments and behaviors by our spouses pass by. The negative comments or behaviors annoy you because they awaken your low self-esteem, which blocks your sunset view of your own true self. If you allow these comments to go by without reacting to them, they pass. Again, if you leave them alone, they go away. The negative feeling that temporarily arose within you also passes. It disappears, and you calm down. How do you attain this state? Just check out your Wheel of

Strengths, realize that you are okay just the way you are, and then let the comment or behavior be. Let it be, and it will pass out of your consciousness. And an argument will be avoided.

You can also do the following exercise to combat your own self-inflicted negative thoughts that plague your view of your true serene self. Imagine that you are standing by the side of a highway, and cars and trucks are passing by. A big ugly eighteen-wheeler comes by. It bothers you, so you wave the truck down, it slows, and you get on it. Then you begin to investigate, asking, "Who owns this monstrosity? What is it doing on my highway? Why is it making so much noise? Why is it taking up two lanes?"

The eighteen-wheel tractor-trailer represents your own negative thoughts: "Why did I marry this person? I could have done better! What is going to happen to my marriage and to my kids? Why is life so hard?" But remember, thoughts have no substance to them. They are merely electric impulses in the brain brought on by fears, old hurts, or unfinished business from childhood. Just like the eighteen-wheeler drives by, the negative thoughts pass. No need to delve into them and tie yourself into knots like a pretzel.

If a negative thought comes into your mind, why let the thought take control over you? Why not sit back and watch the negative thought about your spouse go by? The same is true for a negative comment by your spouse—let it pass without comment. Why get on that truck? Just let it go by. Tell yourself, "I am okay. I have my character and values and Wheel of Strengths. I need not respond or comment negatively." Just maintain your equanimity and serenity, your soul state.

You might think, "Why should I try to maintain my serenity?" You should because you are in control of your own state of mind. You are in control of your view of the beautiful sunset and of the five-lane highway. If negative thoughts or comments come along the horizon or along the highway, why give those thoughts enough power to throw you off track?

After all, don't you believe in free will? Don't you have the power to maintain your vision and view of your own self value? Just because your spouse is feeling bad, why allow her comments to throw you off track of your own sense of validation and worth? Why give your spouse so much power over your emotional state? Take a look at your Wheel of Strengths. Remind yourself of your own good values and character traits. You don't need your spouse's approval to feel good about yourself. You already feel intrinsically validated and worthy. If your spouse also validates and supports you, then great! You will feel even better. But your sense of self does not depend on positive comments by your spouse. Your sense of self depends on you, on your own self-image. That is why it is called <u>self</u> worth. It is your responsibility. If you work on your sense of worth, then you need not disturb the equilibrium by negatively responding to or making a comment about your spouse. Stay with your soul state, shut up, and stay married.

CHAPTER 8 **SHUT UP**
and Use Positive
Self-Talk

When Robert and Allison came to me for counseling two months ago, they were on the verge of divorce. During intensive couple's therapy, we discovered that Robert is highly sensitive and was reacting to every comment made by Allison as if it were an attack, when really no attack existed at all. When I began to see Robert alone for a few sessions, we found that he was suffering from feelings of inadequacy and unworthiness. These feelings were fed by thoughts that plagued him almost every waking hour in the form of an inner dialogue telling him that others were better than him and that he was not a good person, husband, or father. He had lost confidence in his ability to succeed at life.

In this case I used the Wheel of Strengths we discussed in chapter 5. I asked Robert to focus on his strengths and to think positively about himself. I asked him to find the place within himself where his finest, warmest, most caring feelings are centered. I am amazed at how people can change their mood just by consciously thinking positive thoughts. The creation of a positive mind-set can be achieved through mind control. I asked Robert how much time he was spending accessing his "positive self." His suggestion was in the range of 1 percent to 10 percent of the day. This meant that he felt negatively about himself about 90 to 99 percent of the day.

I then asked Robert to symbolically place his negative thoughts in the empty chair in front of him—chair B—and to have his positive self (in Chair A) talk to his negative self. Whenever Robert's negative self was about to speak, I asked Robert to get up and sit in chair B and respond as his negative self. So he went back and forth between chairs as his positive self and negative self entered into a "dialogue" with one another. Here's how the conversation went.

> *Robert's positive self:* You are getting me down, so please leave me alone.
>
> *Robert's negative self:* No way. I am part of you, and I am not leaving.
>
> *Positive self:* Why do you insist on criticizing me?
>
> *Negative self:* I am actually protecting you.
>
> *Positive self:* I don't call putting me down protection.
>
> *Negative self:* By criticizing you, I am keeping you humble. I don't want you to get a swelled head.

Then I came in and helped Robert construct an argument with his negative self. I instructed him to say the following to his negative self:

> *Positive self:* Listen. You are expressing my negative thoughts, which come from my negative self. I want to remind

you that if you want to keep me humble, you have to follow the rules of fair play—just like I have to. So when you correct me, you have to do it in a constructive way. And I have news for you: until now, you have not been speaking to me in accordance with the rules of fair play. You have been putting me down, and this is not acceptable.

Negative self: Too bad!

Positive self: Wrong again. You are a messenger—a representative—of truth, justice, and personal growth. And this attitude will not do. Either you speak to me in accordance with the rules of justice and fair play, or I will have to report you to a higher authority.

Negative self: I didn't realize you felt so strongly about this. I thought that since you just took my comments without responding for so long that you liked the way I spoke to you. It is for your own good, you know.

Positive self: That's enough! Negative talk is not for my own good. I will not accept this anymore. Do you agree to criticize me with positive language and with constructive encouragement?

Negative self: If you insist.

Positive self: I insist.

Negative self: Okay, okay. You don't have to get pushy about it.

Robert practiced this dialogue with me in my office during a few sessions and then got good at catching the negative self, challenging it, and counteracting it. He soon began to counteract the perception in his mind that his wife was criticizing him. She wasn't. He just "heard" her comments as criticism because of the low self-esteem he had developed during childhood. His low self-esteem was his unfinished business from his upbringing. Now Robert and Allison's disagreements no longer escalate into arguments, and they are expecting another child.

You can have a dialogue like this with your negative self, on your own or guided by a counselor or therapist. The idea is that you can put the negative self in its place by realizing that the negative self is not you but is outside of you. That's what you can accomplish by placing the negative self in a chair and having a discussion with it. You, the true self, have the power to control your own inner dialogue.

This technique gives you a way to identify and deal with negative self put-downs and to begin controlling them, instead of allowing them to control you. That is the purpose of therapy. If you have negative internal dialogue and turmoil churning around in your head, then your thoughts control you. When you speak them out loud and analyze them, they become exposed, and you can control your thoughts.

This technique shines new light on your inner dialogue with the negative self. Using it empowers you to engage the negative self and overcome it. Your task is to identify the negative self, find the point it wants you to focus on, and then overcome the test. Tests from the negative self, whether they come in the form of negative thoughts, feeling bad about yourself, or doubting your own abilities, are meant to be dealt with and overcome.

These negative thoughts are sent to help you become more aware of your humanity and your weaknesses and to strengthen you and make you more whole. You can use the negative self to help you grow in character and personality. The fact that you have a negative inner critic does not make you bad—it makes you human. And you can use the positive self to defeat the arguments of the negative self. That is called inner strength.

CHAPTER 9

SHUT UP
and Turn Off
the Autopilot

The negative self gets all the press and publicity. He must have a great agent. All we hear about is how, "My negative self made me do this," My negative self made me do that," "My anger got a hold of me and wouldn't let go," "What can I do? The devil got the better of me." We hear very little from the positive self. We seldom hear, "My positive self really pushed me hard on that one" or "I couldn't help it, my good self really got a hold of me and wouldn't let go."

Why not?

The answer is that we don't naturally get in touch with our positive side. We do naturally give in to the negative self without much effort. But we find it much harder to dig deep and push the "free will" button that activates our positive self, our true self. For that to happen we need to be conscious of our good side. We are painfully aware of our failings and mistakes because the negative voice within us is very vocal. It may well sound like a critical voice from our childhood. We let the positive self remain dormant and passive. This is backwards. We should allow the negative self to remain dormant and push the inner free will button to access the positive self.

Wouldn't it be nice to be able to activate the positive self at will? We can. You see, normally we go through the motions in life while on autopilot. This phenomenon is called living in "automaticity." An example of this state is when the car seems to drive to the office by itself since it goes there every day. We fall into the patterns of inertia rather than a conscious state of decision making.

To break out of this pattern, stop for a moment and access your inner decision-making center. This is the part of you which has the will or desire to do something. If you are able to access this center, you can actually break out of autopilot.

Research has shown that a direct correlation exists between the way we were parented and the way we parent. If our parents were loving and benevolent, then we tend to be the same in our relationships. If our parents acted strict and austere toward each other, then we tend to mirror that behavior. This knowledge can impact the type of relationship you choose to have with your spouse. It will also influence the type of relationship your children choose to have with their own children. If you want to change the way you act then break out of autopilot and be aware that you are not your father and you are not your mother. You are _you_.

Close your eyes for a minute and search your inner self for your best character trait, the part of your inner psyche and personality that feels good about itself (which we discussed in chapter 6). Bring to mind your strongest attribute. Now, while in that mode, compliment your spouse for something he did. Or just for being who she is. In this way you are interacting from free will and conscious choice. You are now out of autopilot. You are taking back control of your life.

CHAPTER 10 SHUT UP

and Stop Making Yourself Angry

When I was a child and was experiencing a "junior moment" (as opposed to a "senior moment"), I would throw a mild tantrum by whining and complaining about being bored and having "nothing to do." My mother would sagely say, "Stop sulking. If you smile, the world smiles with you. Frown, and you frown alone." I would look at my mother and ask, "Just like that? Smile, even though I am bored and depressed? What do I have to smile about? Life is lousy, and I don't feel like smiling. I actually feel like feeling sorry for myself."

Mothers make being happy sound so simple. How can you manipulate your emotions just like that?

The answer is that we are not aware of our own inner strength. We really do have the power to change our mood instantly if we switch into a mind-set of positive thinking. Yes, it is that simple. You can talk yourself out of a bad mood by activating your free will. You can say to yourself, "It is just as easy to allow external events to get me down as it is to say, "I will not allow this setback get me down. I will rise above it!" The key to activating your free will is taking responsibility for your emotions.

When someone upsets us or hurts our feelings, we tend to shift the blame to them by saying, "You are making me angry, upset, annoyed, or frustrated."

The key question we must ask ourselves when someone else is "making us" angry or upset is "Do I believe in free will? If so, then why would I give up my free will to this person and allow this person to determine my mood? Am I a marionette whose strings another person can pull and manipulate? What about my own free choice to control my emotions?

When you allow others to upset you and make you angry, you are really abdicating responsibility for your emotional state. You are giving the other person power over you by becoming enslaved to his or her behavior and comments. You allow whatever the other person says or does to determine and affect your mood and reactions. Why give someone so much power?

In fact, other people are not *making* you do anything. They are not *making* you angry. You are *choosing* to react with anger. <u>You</u> are making *yourself* angry. You can take back control over your own emotional state by exercising control over your reactions. Free will makes you master of your own feelings and liberates you from being emotionally enslaved by others.

This idea applies especially when dealing with spouses. Even though we tend to rely on our spouses for emotional support, we cannot give them control of our emotional state. In this sense we must maintain our own independent emotional identity and take responsibility for our own emotional responses. Emotional independence means that you are in charge of your own mood. Just as your spouse cannot *make* you angry, your spouse is not there to *make* you happy. Only you can do that.

When you get married, you are and you remain a separate individual with a unique personality and set of emotions. Of course, the idea that you "become one" with your spouse is also true but that oneness refers to working together as a unit, giving each other emotional support. But providing emotional support is not the same as giving your spouse an emotional self. Your self does not merge with that of your spouse such that you lose your own identity. You don't become your spouse. Your identity and your mood are your responsibility. Once you discover your own sense of self, you can learn to maintain emotional freedom. Then your emotional self can join with your spouse's emotional self, and you can support each other and grow together. In part 2 we will discuss the ways you can work together emotionally to build a successful loving relationship.

HOW TO CREATE A
GOOD MARRIAGE

PART 2

CHAPTER 11

and Be Grateful

T o nurture a healthy family that thrives with positive
thinking and self-esteem, you need to foster a positive attitude in family members. This self-esteem orientation can
be learned. The secret is to adopt a strengths approach and an "I
can" attitude. This does not mean that everything that happens in
the family is okay. Rather, your attitude should be "let's look for
the positive gifts that my spouse brings to me and our family and
see if I can foster an attitude of gratitude toward my spouse."

The way to develop a positive relationship with your spouse
is to write down the benefits you receive from being married to
your spouse. Let's try an exercise: make a list of the ten things that
you have in your life that you can't or don't want to live without.
My list includes creativity, encouragement from my spouse, my
children, family outings, dinner with the family, and piggyback
rides for the kids up to bed.

Make your own list in the space provided below. Go ahead—
this book is meant to be an interactive exercise in self discovery.
It will take an investment of effort.

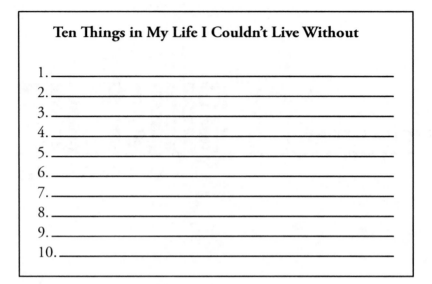

How many of these items relate to your family, home and spouse?

Keep this list by your nightstand, in your car, or in your diary, and review it once a day. Develop a sense of gratitude toward your spouse. This ongoing feeling of gratitude will add a dimension of spirituality and connection to your relationship with your spouse.

Part of the positive thinking approach is that you have to proactively put yourself into a positive mind-set. Otherwise you will find yourself falling automatically into negative thinking by default. Coming to terms with the recession, negotiating politics at work, getting along with neighbors, bringing up children, dealing with in-laws (and of course, spouses) are challenging tasks. A day doesn't go by that doesn't have some disappointment or difficulty. And the problems are much more poignant and earth-shattering than are the positive moments, which are usually fleeting.

Let's try another exercise. Write down five things that are issues or challenges in your life. This should take you about ten seconds. Now, write down five things that are going right in your life. This is probably a lot harder. Let's see, what is going right? This should take you ten seconds to do, but it won't. It will probably take you ten minutes because it is harder to think positive if you are trained to brace yourself for one crisis after another.

When you think and act positively you will create a home atmosphere where the family members will feel secure and this will, in turn, be more conducive to their physical and emotional health. That's why you have to push and train yourself and your family to use the gratitude approach. Make it a family project to have each family member write five things on a poster for which each is grateful, and put the poster on the wall in the kitchen. This gratitude poster will wake you up when you have breakfast and put you in a mode of positive awareness and happiness.

At the dinner table, ask each family member to share a positive or happy moment that they experienced that day. Ask them to elaborate on that event and give them feedback. This will foster a positive and light atmosphere in the home. If nothing significantly positive happened that day then ask them to share something that was challenging for them today. Discuss it and empathize with their feelings. This will foster emotional openness and will facilitate emotional support in the family. When family members share mutual feelings, that will develop a sense of togetherness and trust. When people open up about their feelings, their relationship is strengthened. In this way, an ethos of positivity will develop in the family.

CHAPTER 12 # SHUT UP
and Listen

When I was studying to become a rabbi in Jerusalem, my teacher, Rabbi Naftoli Kaplan, would look intensely at each of us when we asked a question on the Talmud. I remember how he would focus on my face, trying to understand my question as if he were looking into my mind. It made a deep impression on me that such a scholar would give my simple questions so much attention and value.

When I would get home at night and have dinner with my wife, she would ask me questions about my day and my studies, and we would discuss our plans and the issues of the day. Often, I would be looking in a Talmudic book as she spoke to me, trying not to waste precious time. I figured I could listen with one ear to my wife's mundane concerns like the budget, shopping, the baby's cold, and the Sabbath guest list while focusing on the lofty and spiritual matters contained in the Talmud with the other ear. One night my wife picked up the book, gently closed it, and said, "Is this how your teacher talks to his wife?"

My thoughts immediately went to my teacher's intensity when he listened to my questions. I thought, "My teacher is a giant scholar and he gives me, a fledgling student, his full time and attention. And here my wife and I are equals and I don't have time to give her my undivided attention?"

I still think about this contrast twenty years later. When my wife comes to sit next to me as I work at my computer, she waits until I remember my teacher's focus and intensity. She refuses to talk to me while I am on the computer. She wants, deserves, and waits for my full attention.

Giving someone your full attention starts with listening. After all, listening is 50 percent of the art of communication. The great psychologist, Carl Rogers, created a valuable approach to listening called the Person-Centered approach.[2] The technique consists of mirroring and reflecting back to the spouse or child what he has said, for example, "Oh, you want me to read you a book?" or "You would like me to help me with your homework," or "You are having difficulty organizing the carpool. That must be frustrating." In this way you acknowledge and validate the presence and feelings of the other person. This approach is called active listening and will give the other person the feeling that you are there for them.

Why is undivided attention so important to us? When someone is focused on us and our needs, we feel gratified and taken care of. Attentive listening makes us feel recognized and valued. This attention touches our inner sense of self. Our inner sense of value and self-worth is our own responsibility. However, if you want to really connect with your spouse, giving her undivided focus and attention will validate and nurture her essence and make her emotionally receptive to you.

CHAPTER 13

and Stop Lecturing

Students at school and children at home share one complaint: "Don't tell me what to do." As soon as they hear a "Do this, and don't do that" tone of voice, they shut down. They look down sheepishly or roll their eyes. They take bets as to how long the current harangue is going to take. They doodle or think about something else. Human beings under eighteen seem to be hard-wired with a natural opposition to authority.

The problem is that parents and teachers are hard-wired to exert authority. So as families we are in a no-win situation. The authority figures are stuck in the mode of disciplining their charges, not so much out of a need to teach, but out of self-defense. As parents we need to run a tight ship and keep the family enterprise moving with its pressures of carpools, lunches, bedtime, and squeezing in quality time. As teachers we need to maintain discipline in the classroom for fear of losing control of the march toward curriculum completion. In short, our default position as adults is to tell people what to do—and often.

But how else are we going to get our children and students to get it right? Isn't it incumbent on us as parents and teachers to discipline our children and students so that they will eventually make the right choices? The psychology of motivation teaches us that the best way to get a student or child to dedicate themselves to our way of life is with inspiration and positivity rather than rebuke and discipline.

Have you ever tried to get an unruly child to behave? No matter how much you admonish, threaten, or go "head to head" with the child, you do not achieve the desired result. Children do not respond to criticism for the same reason that you and I do not like to like to receive criticism or lectures from our spouses. We do not grow through rebuke. We learn through our own painful mistakes, but we do not learn from rebuke from others because verbal criticism provides no incentive for growth. It just breeds resentment and creates emotional distance.

Children will want to follow your instruction when you provide them with positive reinforcement and encourage their appropriate behavior. When you see a positive act, then comment on it and praise it. Then the child will have an incentive to repeat that behavior. For example, if the child cleared away only one plate from the table instead of all the plates, you could say, "That was very responsible of you to clear away your plate," instead of, "What about the other plates?" This way the child will feel encouraged and may well come back for more. If instead you say, "You only cleared away one plate! Are you the only person who lives here?" your child will say to herself, "Nothing I ever do is recognized. My contribution is never good enough." The child will eventually internalize the mind-set that not only are her actions not good enough, but also that she, herself, is not good enough. This atmosphere will hardly inspire greater cooperation in the future or healthy self-esteem.

Parents often push children to behave and "fly right" with tough-love comments like the following: "Tuck in your shirt," "Don't be so lazy," "Stop being so inconsiderate," "You are being mean," "If your head wasn't screwed on, it would fall off," "Oh, here comes our math genius!" "Will you clean up your room already?" "How many times do I have to remind you to make your lunch?" "Get to bed, now!", "Come on lazy bones, get up already," "You're being selfish!" "Stop being so pushy!"

How many of these comments do we direct toward our children per day? Three, five, ten? Or is it one long stream of such comments all day long? Of course, they are justified because we have to keep our children in line and keep our ship afloat, right? Let's be conservative and say that we make five such comments to our children per day. That would be thirty five such comments per week or 1,820 such comments per year, which would amount to 18,200 negative comments by the time the child is ten years old! And you still don't understand why your child feels bad about herself and keeps putting herself down. Oh, really?

As parents and teachers, we need to become aware of the educational and developmental fact that we create children's sense of self through the comments, feedback, and body language we use when we interact with them. We have that power because developmentally, a child doesn't have a sense of self other than the one we give them. For example, if you say to your child, "You are kind, giving, sensitive, caring, conscientious, and responsible," then the child will say to herself, "I did not know that about myself." Your child trusts the significant authority figures in his life to tell him the truth about himself and his world. You have the power to create a positive self-image or a negative self-image in your children and students, and you must use that power wisely.

With your spouse, how many negative comments or corrections do you feel are appropriate for you to receive per day? Is it okay if every second comment is negative? How about every third comment? How about every fifth comment? The truth is that any amount of lectures, criticisms, or negativity sours the tone of the relationship. And besides, these criticisms never work because they do not fit into the incentive and motivation system of the human psyche.

If you don't want to receive such criticism then stop correcting your spouse because it simply will not get your spouse to comply with your request. It will make him resist, feel distant from you and will breed resentment. And it certainly won't be conducive to intimacy.

Only warmth and positivity will make your spouse want to be close to you, emotionally or physically. In other words, if you shut up, you will stay married.

CHAPTER 14 # SHUT UP

and Learn
From Adversity

Y ou may say to yourself, "Why is everything so hard for me? Why does life deal me the worst of situations? Why does everyone seem to reject me? Why is my marriage so difficult? Don't I deserve a little happiness?" Self-talk like this can destroy your self-confidence and self-esteem and prevent you from developing a meaningful relationship with your world.

The individual and his universe exist in a constant tense battle of wills: many of us think, "the universe and I don't quite see eye to eye." Whether physical illness, financial problems, or difficulty in marriage, the world seems to put up impenetrable roadblocks to our attempts at achieving happiness and fulfillment.

The universe is not rejecting you with these obstacles, even though you may feel that way. The opposite is true. If the universe was not interested in your development, it would not take the time to challenge you. It would simply let you go merrily on your way. Even though we would like the universe to pay less attention to us and let us be, going through life without challenges is not the essence of real living.

Real living consists of encountering obstacles and delving into our personal strengths and resources in order to meet challenges and grow through the process. Couldn't the universe be designed whereby we could grow from positive events and forgo the challenges? Yes—but that kind of system would not have led to our ultimate benefit.

Our natural reaction to life's challenges is one of humility and modesty. Or you might call it despair. Each of us has said at least once:

- I can't do this.
- This is too much for me.
- I can't take it anymore.
- I can't go on.
- Life is not fair.

Of course life has difficult moments and challenges, and of course you are going to feel that you would like to throw in the towel at times. That feeling is your emotional self giving an automatic, instinctive response of self-defense and self-preservation. Yet, those moments are precisely when you must dig deep and access your true self. The challenge is tailor-made for you to reach for your Wheel of Strengths and bring out your best character traits. When you are pushed up against the wall, your true identity is revealed.

Accessing the true self takes tremendous personal fortitude and inner strength. This is itself the purpose of life—to become the best person you can become. The challenge has been sent to you to help you actualize your potential. The fulfillment of your life's purpose then, by definition, cannot be easy. You have been sent into this world to meet life's challenges. Marriage is one of those challenges. It is designed to help each spouse grow into the best person each can become. That process takes commitment, effort and perseverance.

One more question, of course, remains: why does the world work this way? Why does personal growth only happen through travail and sometimes painful suffering? Could we not live in a world where we could grow through pleasurable experiences and ease?

The answer lies in the following story. A boy comes upon a butterfly emerging from its cocoon. He sees the nascent butterfly struggling. The cocoon flails back and forth as the butterfly struggles to set itself free. The boy has pity on the painful struggle of the butterfly and cuts open the cocoon. The butterfly is now free. Moments later the boy sees the butterfly, and it is limping. He had hoped to watch it spread its orange and black Monarch wings and fly on its life's journey. Instead it is in pain. Its wings are glued shut. It cannot move. It soon dies.

In the end, the struggle of the butterfly was necessary for its wings to become healthy. The struggle was actually strengthening its wings and making them ready for the winds of life. Without enduring the struggle required to emerge from the cocoon, the butterfly could not gain the strength it needed to fly to freedom. Struggle and travail were essential for its survival.

Everything we see in this world is a metaphor from which we can learn life lessons. The caterpillar's transformation from its first world of slow creeping, plodding, and crawling on small legs is its challenge. The journey to its life fulfillment requires a stay in a cocoon and a dramatic transformation. The only way the caterpillar can become a butterfly is through struggle—the travail that prepares it for its renewed existence.

Personal challenges are not pleasant. We would all like life to go smoothly, our marriage to work easily, and our children to be low maintenance. But then life would not get us to our goal, which is personal growth. We usually only grow when we are pressed. When we are challenged, our best character traits are activated. When the chips are down, we deliver. But if we were not challenged, many of our talents and strengths would remain dormant. The purpose of life is to develop into the most caring, giving, and sensitive person we can become. We must therefore make friends with our challenges, including the challenges in marriage, and work through them. Through the process of working out our marriage issues, we will develop our values and character and become the best person we can become.

CHAPTER 15 # SHUT UP
and Transform Yourself

my ten-year-old daughter was walking from our next-door neighbor's house toward our home. When she came through the door, she said: "It is so amazing! I was paying attention to my legs for eleven seconds as I walked home, and I said, "Wow, my legs work! They go up and down and make me move!" I said, "Ah, you have become aware that you are actually alive!"

Too often, however, we require adversity, illness, or a tragedy to remind us to appreciate the gift of life. Do we only appreciate something when we are about to lose it? Do we only take our lives seriously when we are forced to justify our existence? Does life only become meaningful when our lives are on the line?

Take for example the sad case of someone who has been diagnosed with a terminal illness. His doctor tells him that he has six months to live. He sadly puts his affairs in order and prepares for the end. At the end of six months, the doctor calls him in and tells him that the illness has miraculously disappeared and that he will live. How does the patient react? He is overjoyed beyond words.

He feels a sense of exhilaration and euphoria. He is bursting with joy. Everything he sees, touches, tastes, hears, and smells takes on great and appreciated significance. The sun shines! The sky is really blue! The air smells so fresh! The traffic on the way home is music to his ears. He now loves traffic jams. They give him time to look at the wonders of life all around him. He begins to feel alive—much more richly alive than he did before.

So what does this man have that we don't? He appreciates his life, and we take ours for granted. He also took his life for granted until he almost lost it. Do we have to be pressed against the wall and almost lose what we love to begin to truly appreciate what we have? It appears that is the way we usually operate. We become desensitized to the magic of life and we live on automatic pilot.

We have bought into the idea in the Constitution that we have a "right to life, liberty, and the pursuit of happiness." We define "right" as a privilege that we are entitled to because we have worked for it and earned it. However, we did not work for our right to be alive. We were given life as a free gift. Can we live on this level of awareness? Or does this awareness only kick in as a default mode when we witness tragedy and realize that "It could have been me?"

Awareness of the fact that your life is a gift is humbling. You feel humbled that you have been given the gift of life, and at the same time, you feel inspired that you have the opportunity to make a unique contribution to society. This next story illustrates the combination of uniqueness and humility.

A teacher of mine who lives in Jerusalem, Rabbi Cardozo, tells the story of his neighbor, a member of the Jerusalem Symphony Orchestra, who was practicing his violin in preparation for a performance of Mozart's Fifth Symphony. The rabbi enjoyed his neighbor's music as background for his own writing. One evening the violinist knocked on the rabbi's door and offered him two tickets to attend the performance of Mozart's Fifth at the home of Israel's president featuring the world-famous virtuoso, Itzhak Perlman. It was the least he could do, said the violinist, for having put the rabbi through three months of practice.

The rabbi came back home after the performance, knocked on the violinist's door, and said, "I have listened to you practice this piece for three months and I thought I knew it by heart. How come I could not recognize the piece as played by Itzhak Perlman?" The violinist answered, "I won't tell you the answer until you come hear Sir Yehudi Menuhin play the same piece at the Jerusalem Conference Center in three weeks' time." The rabbi agreed and attended the second performance, and when he heard Sir Yehudi Menuhin play Mozart's Fifth differently than Itzhak Perlman, he came up with his own answer: each musician brought his own interpretation to the music based on his own unique life experience. Each soloist played the same notes— he wouldn't dare change the musical score —but each expressed his own individuality based on his personal passion.

The individuality and passion of each person's life experience can be brought to bear on the way in which each person decides to lead his life. Therein lies our individuality and unique creativity. Each person brings his own personal melody and passion to the journey we call life. No two people act the same way or with the same emphasis and intensity. Each of us has his own unique strengths and weaknesses and his own unique life challenges.

The same is true with our personal growth. Each person must pay attention to the resistance that our negative self puts up in order to push us to overcome our obstacles. When we want to discover how we are supposed to grow in character, we need only look for the mistake or character flaw that we constantly fall prey to. Overcoming that fault is the reason we were sent into the world.

If you keep stumbling over the same mistake, wake up and pay attention. For example, if you are always losing your temper with your spouse, you are always impatient, or you are always cutting someone off in mid-sentence and this flaw really bothers you, then your soul is "speaking to you," saying, "Overcoming this fault is your mission. Fix this." Thus, each of us is challenged with a unique inclination toward a particular type of mistake, and we have to become attuned to this inclination in order to discover what to work on in our character development.

In the same way, your spouse has been sent to you as a tailor-made partner to help you grow in character and become the best person you can become. Instead of complaining about, rejecting, or criticizing your spouse, your job is to shut up and stay married. This does not mean staying in an unhealthy marriage. Rather, shutting up means looking into your own psyche and your own inner self and discovering how you can grow into a better spouse, parent and person.

When you hear that your spouse was hurt by a comment you made, instead of lashing out and retaliating, you must learn to shut up and look inside yourself to see how you can grow from the mistake. Putting your spouse down because you were hurt by her comment would be missing the point. It would be shifting the blame onto her rather than taking personal responsibility for your own growth.

You must learn to shut up and stay married so that you can work on your own self, grow in character and values, and become the best person you can become. That is the purpose of life. Work with your spouse by working through the issues, and allow your marriage to help you achieve your life's purpose.

HOW TO CREATE A HAPPY FAMILY

PART 3

CHAPTER 16 # SHUT UP

and Empower Your Children

A great twelfth-century Talmudic philosopher, Maimonides, once taught that the world is precariously balanced between good and bad, success and failure. Maimonides says that each act of ours must be weighed and measured carefully because each action can tip our own personal moral scale, and the scale of the entire universe, for good or for bad. The fate of the world is in our hands: one good act will tip the world's scale and its judgment for the good, and one negative act can tip the world's scale toward negativity. You and I have tremendous power and responsibility to affect the entire spiritual balance of the world.

This concept is both scary and empowering. It's all a question of attitude. Do you look at yourself as a miniscule speck of dust in the universe who can ruin the whole world with one negative comment to your spouse or one criticism of your child? Or do you look at yourself as an empowered being who can say one positive comment to your spouse or one word of praise to your child that can build them up—and the entire world with them?

The concept that we have the power to affect and influence the world can be explained to children on a level that they can appreciate. You can teach children that their actions make a difference. For example, you can have them plant a lima bean seed in a glass and watch it grow, day by day. You can then implant in them the awareness that <u>they</u> planted the seed and <u>they</u> facilitated its growth. Their actions facilitate change.

You can also empower your children with the idea that they are in control of making good choices. If they do, they will be expressing their own true selves. You can say to your child, "You are choosing to act in a positive manner right now. I am proud of you."

But what if your child chooses to exercise his free will negatively? Does that make him bad? No. This is the most important rule of self-esteem parenting. It is taught to parents by a little angel on the night before their first child is born. After all, how do you transform yourself from a couple into a family overnight? What more do you know after you have been blessed with a child?

The key message in this Parenting 101 course is to never say to your child, "Bad girl" or "Bad boy." Rather, say, "You are worthy. You have value that can never be taken from you. Your soul state is always intact. What you are choosing to do right now is unacceptable. You are exercising your free will in a manner that is not worthy of a fine person like you."

In this way you are differentiating between the child as a person and the child's actions. The child's worth is never questioned or put at risk. The child is a reflection of goodness. Her current choices may be creating negative energy, but she can choose to make positive choices with her next expression of free will.

You can maintain children's self-esteem while disciplining them with a positive strategy that will inspire them to rise to the occasion and improve their behavior. You can discipline from a perspective of positivity and encouragement rather than a place of negativity and heavy-handedness. Think about it. Which approach would motivate *you* to change for the better?

CHAPTER 17

SHUT UP

and Smile

Imagine yourself in the kitchen in the midst of your family "happy hour." You know—the 5:00 p.m. to 7:00 p.m. window when the children come home from school clamoring for a snack, dinner is boiling over on the stove, the baby needs to be fed, the phone is ringing with the doctor calling back about your older child, homework needs to be supervised, your mother-in-law is calling as to why no one called her to thank her for the birthday card—a normal day in the life. (I don't have to tell you, right?) You are about to lose control because your teenager is on the other line schmoozing when he could be helping, and your wife called and said that she is coming home late. So what now?

The antidote is simple—the art of smiling.

A smile is an expression of acceptance. It is the body language of validation and value. Even more than words, a facial expression communicates our true feelings. You may say, "I love you," but when you do it with a scowl and hurriedly, the person does not believe you.

Smiling is important because our children reflect our moods. To see how, consider a client of mine who was trying to understand why he had a perpetual negative attitude toward everything. In the workplace, with family, or at social occasions, he was inevitably the naysayer, pouring cold water on any new idea and pointing out the negatives in people. He was the ultimate pessimist. In our sessions he revealed that he had lost his father when he was two years old and that his mother raised him and his sister, doing an admirable job at single parenting.

When I brought his mother into my office for family counseling, she recalled that her son had always had a sad look on his face in his childhood, "even in the family photographs while he was in the stroller." I asked about how she coped raising two children on her own, and she related that she was very bitter about her situation. She said, "It was very hard. I cried all the time at my miserable fate of loneliness."

I then suggested to my client that his mother may well have communicated her negative attitude and pain to her children in her interactions with them. She admitted that no doubt she did, and I said, "I suppose it stands to reason that your son's face reflected your pain and sadness." That was an important "ahah" moment of realization for mother and son.

Like this son, our children reflect our moods. Therefore, we are responsible for creating a happy childhood for our children by maintaining our own positive mood and by using the art of smiling. If a mother comes home from work and is nervous and unapproachable, saying, "Mommy had a tough day," she puts a damper on the atmosphere of the home. On the other hand, if you turn your back on the world's "issues" when you walk toward your front door and you enter your home smiling, you can uplift the mood of your home.

I know what you're saying to yourself: "But I did have a really bad day, and I don't feel like smiling. And my kids have to see me cope with sadness too." True. But they shouldn't have to see you in that mode as a general rule—only as an exception. Your general mood and mode of relating to your spouse and children must be one of happiness because your face and attitude are in the public domain. You can cope with personal sadness by making an appointment with yourself for later on that evening after the kids are in bed to review, discuss, and work through the painful issue. But for now you need to set aside your own needs and ego in order to cater, with a smile, to the emotional needs of your spouse and children. In this way you can create a positive environment in which your family members' sense of self can thrive.

CHAPTER 18 # SHUT UP

and Motivate Your Children to Change

When family life is going well, being a supportive parent, is easy. The children are in the "zone" and make you look like a parenting professional. What happens, however, when family life gets stuck and in a rut? What do you do when one of your children won't get up on time, won't keep his room clean, doesn't exert enough effort at school, and is constantly fighting with his siblings? You would like to find something good about him to praise, but quite frankly you don't see much that's going right! You are at your wit's end, and your child's behavior is testing your patience severely. Your own self-esteem plummets, along with that of your child. Now what?

The technique you can try when all seems bleak is to turn the problem behavior into a goal. If mornings are tough, then "making mornings smooth" becomes your goal. If homework is not getting done, then "homework success" becomes your goal. If fighting with siblings is creating havoc, then peacemaking becomes your goal. Yet how do you reach these elusive goals?

None of your coaxing, discipline, or guilt trips have worked. So where to now?

The key to parenting success is to realize that behavior will never change with discipline, lectures, warnings, punishments, pleadings, or time-outs. These techniques just breed resentment. (By the way, these aren't techniques; they are really knee-jerk reactions.) The way to promote cooperative behavior is to recognize, praise, and reward the behaviors that you would like to see repeated. Positive feedback on positive behavior will foster more of that behavior.

This positive feedback concept requires a system. Take the child aside and tell her that in life we are all trying to improve ourselves, that you, as a parent, are always trying to learn more about parenting and life so that you can grow. Tell her that, in fact, the purpose of life is to improve our character. Ask her in what way she would like to improve or grow. Lead her to the "goal" behavior and tell her that you and she are going to start a Success Chart whereby she will earn tickets as she works toward her goals. If she gets 30 tickets for the week, she will earn a prize that you can negotiate.

Take the target behavior and break it down into five or six small realizable steps. For example, cleaning her room would be broken down into picking up clothes, making the bed, and so on. List the steps in the form of a chart like the one below.

MEAGAN'S SUCCESS CHART							
	S	M	T	W	Th	F	S
Pick up clothes							
Put clothes in hamper							
Hang up nice clothes							
Make bed							
Sweep floor							
Throw away rubbish							

When you want to work on certain interpersonal behaviors choose the target behaviors that apply to your child. Such a chart would look like the one below.

JONATHAN'S SUCCESS CHART							
	S	M	T	W	Th	F	S
Says: "I am angry" instead of hitting							
Is helpful to brother							
Walks away from a fight							
Helps Mom							
Speaks respectfully							

The purpose of these charts is to reward positive behavior as it happens. A ticket should be handed to your child as soon as a positive behavior is observed. If there are two parents both should participate in this system by giving tickets. And the ticket should be given with warm, positive verbal feedback. The child is responsible for keeping tickets in a safe place and informing her parent when she has earned enough tickets to receive a prize.

Significant negative behavior receives a consequence. The consequence must be a logical fit to respond to the particular negative behavior. If a child hits you or another child, he gets a "hands" consequence; for example, he loses computer time or the use of a game. The length of time of the removal of the privilege depends on the age of the child and the severity of the behavior. If a child kicks another child she receives a "foot" consequence; for example the child loses the privilege of an outing with her parent or the use of her inline skates or skateboard (for an hour, two hours, or a day.) If your child speaks disrespectfully, he receives a "mouth" consequence; for example he loses a cookie or a chips treat in his lunch at school the next day.

By matching the consequence to the behavior, you are teaching your child that a direct correlation exists between her behavior and its ramifications. Giving the consequence without emotion or anger is essential. This will remove the emotional power struggle involved in the child trying to provoke you with her behavior. The consequence system is set up as part of your family system. Tantrums or acting out won't lessen the consequence. The consequence will teach her to think twice before acting impulsively.

When you see negative behavior brewing, you can say to your child, "You have a choice: you can earn tickets, or you can get a consequence. The choice is yours. I am sure you will make the right choice." Then walk away. This will show the child that you have confidence that she can choose wisely and control her behavior. In this way you can give a warning before the consequence is imposed so that your child has a chance to get out of her instinctive mode and think her actions through before reacting impulsively. And that is the point: to give your child a chance to catch his breath, access his free will, and activate his true self.

For positive behavior, four or five tickets can be awarded each day for a possible total of about thirty tickets for the week. If the child achieves the goal by the end of the week, the prize should be awarded on the day you tally the tickets. That shows that you follow through on your promises and that good behavior does have immediate positive consequences. If a child fails to achieve the stated goal, you can award a lesser prize to recognize the child's effort.

Don't be worried that the child will always need these rewards to keep her on track. The targeted behavior will take eight to ten weeks to become integrated in the child's psyche and mode of operating. Once it is part of her, she will say, "I don't need that chart anymore." You may want to reinstate the chart system for a big goal at a later date or if the targeted behavior starts slipping. For example, your child may say, "How many tickets do I need to earn to get a doll house (or a baseball glove)?" Such a large prize may require one hundred tickets or more. I have one client who had to earn one thousand tickets to earn a three-day trip to Florida with her mother. During the points program, she grew tremendously, and the emotional bond between mother and daughter got stronger due to the constant positive feedback that the mother gave to her daughter.

Many parents have said to me that charts don't work. But when I ask, "How long did you use the chart?" they answer, "I tried it for two weeks, but when I saw it didn't work, I gave up." The chart didn't work because they were looking for immediate results, and instant results are not possible when you are trying to change ingrained behaviors. Perseverance and patience are a must. Consistency in parenting will make the system work.

What is the objective of this program of behavior modification? The goal is something more than simply changing the child's behaviors. It is to empower the child by showing him that he has the personal power and free will to achieve his own destiny and to improve the quality of his own life.

Through this ticket system you are trying to restore your child's power of choice to regain control over his actions. The particular challenging "junior moment," be it a sibling argument, homework frustration, or a discipline issue, may have temporarily activated his ego and controlled his reactions. Once you acknowledge your child's emotional distress and remind him that you understand his frustration— and that he can rise above it— you can remind the child that he has the free will to overcome his automatic impulsive response. Rather than react with your own frustration and anger to the child's behavior, you can dig deep, access your own true self, and ask the child to become aware of his autopilot response.

The chart system trains the child that he has the power to break out of the automatic response and to free himself by reacting with his true self.

Over time, when you reward a child for using her soul-state (which is synonymous with her true self) response she will learn to get in touch with this higher self and then learn to consciously activate it. This system will enable a child to learn about empathy and compassion and develop sensitivity to the feelings of others. Of course, time and effort are required for a child to develop a sense of compassion and empathy, but it is worth the effort because eventually this child will grow into adulthood and will be better prepared to succeed in marriage.

CHAPTER 19 SHUT UP
and Discover Your Children's Strengths

As parents we need to turn off the negative, critical mode and switch to the positive mode. In other words, shut off the criticism. We can do this by changing the atmosphere and ethos of the family. The Wheel of Strengths can be one of the vehicles for this change.

The Wheel of Strengths can be made into a family project. Every person in the family should have one, even children as young as five. Our responsibility as parents is to help children discover who they are and what their strengths are. When we give children specific feedback, we are helping to create their identity.

Saying to a child, "You're great!" or "That was terrific," or "You're wonderful," is not enough. First of all, she won't believe you because her experience in school and socially is that she makes mistakes and that she is not that terrific. Second, the child won't be able to repeat that comment to herself, consciously or subconsciously. No child will walk around saying to herself, "I am terrific."

What we need to do is make specific and targeted comments that the child will believe, learn from, and be able to repeat to himself. For example, "You cleaned up your room. That was very responsible of you," or, "You were helpful to your sister. That was considerate," or, "You gave up your turn to your brother. You really know how to be a giver." Not only will specific comments like these build your child's self-esteem, they will actually build his identity and true self. They will also teach the child about character development.

Let us say that you have a child with Attention Deficit Disorder (ADD) or a learning disability such as an auditory processing problem who has difficulty absorbing information. He may want to learn, but cannot learn as well as others. How can he have self-esteem despite receiving low grades? The answer is that a child is much more than his academic performance. In school, children are mostly graded by academic performance. Most of elementary school and even high school curricula stress the development of a child's memory capacity—remembering facts, figures and dates. But a child's personality also includes the desire to learn, character, social skills, extracurricular interests, and spirituality. These traits can be seen in the Wheel of Strengths which you can create with your child. Show your child that he is much more than his grades in school.

Children can excel in sports, art, and other extracurricular endeavors, and one of the keys to developing self-esteem in a child who has a learning challenge is to find an area—in music, art, dance, drama, woodworking, electronics, or other activity—where the child can excel and express her creative self. The child, parents, teachers, and advisors should brainstorm together to discover the creative field of excellence that each child has within her. If you haven't found it, then you haven't looked hard enough. Every child has a yearning to learn, and you must explore and discover your child's unique pathway early on in order to channel it into an area where the child can feel unique and accomplished.

CHAPTER 20   SHUT UP

in Front of
Your Children

When you are not getting what you want from your marriage, when you and your spouse are constantly at each other, and you are feeling trapped in an unhappy marriage, you tend to look for allies to support your cause. Turning to a close friend for emotional support is a good idea. However, the most convenient allies to whom you may mistakenly turn, are your children. This happens for two reasons. First, they are close at hand. Second, you may feel that you can get through to your spouse by complaining to the children. You think that if your spouse hears that you are so upset that you are turning to your children, then perhaps your spouse will wake up and change.

In psychological terms this phenomenon is called "triangulation." You attempt to make a triangle by finding an ally to take your side. Then, you and your child are at two points of the triangle, and you feel you can better defend yourself against the last point of the triangle—your spouse. You don't necessarily do this on purpose to get back at your spouse—you gravitate toward this approach naturally because you are desperate.

You make comments to your children like:

- Your father is so irritating. I hope you are seeing what not do when you become a husband.
- Your mother just doesn't understand me. You understand me better.
- You are a much kinder person than your father.
- You are a much better housekeeper than your mother.
- I find that I can relate to you better than your father.

These comments are attempts to psychologically open up to your child. And these comments are extremely damaging to your child. First, they make your child into your friend and confidante, changing the dynamic of your parent-child relationship. Your children do not want to be your friend! They need to know that you can look after them as a parent protects a child. Once you take your children into your confidence, you are putting them on the same level as you. This is unsettling for them because they feel that now they need to take care of <u>you</u>. This sense of responsibility causes them to feel insecure because it confuses them as to their identity. They say to themselves, "I thought I was a kid. Now I don't know who I am—a friend to my parent, sister to my parent, or therapist to my parent. Who am I?"

Even more damaging is the impression left in the mind of the child that maybe she is your spouse. The reason your child thinks this is because you put the child in an untenable and awkward position by treating her like your equal, your partner, your emotional support. This undermines the trust in the relationship. Essentially, this behavior is a breach of trust. The parent-child relationship becomes unclear and skewed, and in turn the relationship with your spouse becomes more strained and distanced. So you must remember to shut up in front of your children and stay married.

The appropriate person to turn to when you and your spouse are in trouble is an impartial therapist. A therapist can teach you both how to be emotionally supportive and how to give each other what you both need, which is understanding on an adult-to-adult level. Turning to a friend for emotional support is okay in the short term. You need friends to understand you. But if you want to repair the issues in the marriage, you must learn techniques and new communication skills. These can be learned from a trained professional.

CHAPTER 21

SHUT UP

and Survive the Thunderstorms

There are only two core emotions from which all others flow: love and fear. Love is the wellspring for expressions of kindness and feelings of happiness, positivity, encouragement, serenity, and well-being. If you are feeling loved, then you can express love. The source in your soul for your expressions of love is a feeling that you are accepted, validated, and appreciated. In other words, if you feel that you are recognized as a person of value and worth, then you can interact with others from inner strength and confidence. If members of your family interact with you and others with positive feelings and joy, then you know that internally, they are feeling accepted and loved.

On the other end of the spectrum is fear. Fear generates feelings of self-centeredness, egotism, criticism, sadness, negativity, turmoil, and anger. If you are feeling unaccepted you'll find it difficult accepting others. The source of expressions of anger and negativity is a feeling that you are not being appreciated and validated. If you do not feel that others recognize that you are a person of substance and worth, you will be forced into a defensive position. You will interact with others with suspicion, paranoia, and irritability. The source in your soul of this feeling of negativity and anger is a fear that you lack value, a feeling of low self-esteem. If you are not feeling valued, you can hardly value others. Hence you act out with abrasiveness and anger.

Therefore, whenever you are on the receiving end of criticism, anger, or negativity, stop yourself from reacting in the moment. Not only will this escalate the situation, it will not get to the core of the problem. In this situation, if you understand the "self" issues that are at play, then you will stop and ask yourself, "In what way is this person not feeling accepted or validated?"

When a child or a spouse is exhibiting negativity or criticism, you must see through the behavior and discover its core: a feeling of fear. When someone is upset or angry, how can the source of that anger be fear? The fear is a fear of not being understood, accepted, or validated. This is an existential fear that someone's person or life is not valuable or worthy.

When we witness the negative or critical behavior of a child or spouse, we tend to get upset and frustrated and then lose control. We get frustrated by their irritability and we answer back, which makes the situation worse. The argument escalates and spirals out of control. Isn't it amazing how a simple misunderstanding can be blown out of proportion?

Here is a simple but profound technique that can help you understand your child or spouse and get to the core of the matter. It's called the Thunderstorm Model. When a child witnesses lightning and thunder, her reaction is usually one of fear. She might cry and even hide under the covers or under the table. What is your response to your child's fear? Do you reprimand her for her fear and tell her to get over it? No. You reach out to her and comfort her. You soothe her and show her love and security.

Let's look at it from a psychological perspective. When you are late for an appointment with me, I may get angry at you.

What is behind my anger? Psychologically, I am experiencing a fear that I am not worthy or valuable enough for you to exert sufficient energy and effort to come to the meeting on time. I may say to myself, "Am I not worth the effort? If I was more important, you would have come on time." This perception— my feeling not good enough —takes place in my subconscious mind. I may not even be aware of it consciously. My emotional response is anger, but subconsciously I am questioning my sense of value. Underlying my anger is a fear that I am not valuable enough.

This is precisely what happens when a child or spouse is feeling existentially threatened. His feeling of value or validation as a person of worth has been threatened, and he reacts with negativity, anger, criticism, or even a tantrum. When this happens, remember the Thunderstorm Model. You can remedy the situation by understanding that the individual is experiencing a sense of fear and a lack of inner confidence about his core value. In the case of a child, a sibling may have put him down or may seem to be getting more attention than him. In the case of a spouse who is expressing anger, she may be feeling misunderstood, embarrassed, hurt or criticized.

In either case, child or adult, the person experiences the same type of fear as a child in a thunderstorm. He needs reassurance, not criticism. He needs acceptance, not a lecture or reprimand. People who are displaying anger or negativity need warmth, validation, and emotional support. Ask what happened. You can say, "You must be feeling upset. I am sorry that happened. I think you are a good person even though you feel bad."

Empathize with the person's feelings, and validate them without sounding patronizing or condescending. She is probably feeling left out or that she is not being understood. Sit down, reconnect and give her a sense that you appreciate her intrinsic value. That is the key to understanding the true self of the other person. You can restore someone to positive thinking and emotional equilibrium with validation and acceptance. The expression of love, the most basic and essential emotion, will revive the person's sense of self and get her back on track.

CHAPTER 22

SHUT UP

and Lighten Up

When you took your first steps as a toddler, you wobbled tentatively and finally let go of the couch for the first time. Just as you tottered out into the middle of the room, your father opened his arms and beckoned you to keep walking toward him. Remember? And then (and here is the problem), just as you moved forward, flailing and tumbling toward him, he moved back! Now, why would a loving father do that? The answer, of course, is that he wanted you to learn to walk. He wanted you to push yourself and go beyond your current limits and achieve more.

When you reflect on your sense of self, you would do well to look back at the process of growth that you have achieved over the years. You should not allow yourself to be disheartened by any particular mistake or failing. Look back at how far you have come and how you approached this same issue many years before. Appreciate that your method of approaching the particular challenge has, in all likelihood, changed, and that you now deal with it more maturely and prudently. Your method may not yet be perfect, but lighten up on your self-criticism and appreciate how far you have come.

So too, should you lighten up when you guide and interact with your children. Encourage them to look back at how they used to deal with a problem and how they have improved.

There is a difference between a child's self and his actions. Even if what he has done is less than desirable, don't let anything undermine his true self—his intrinsic value. You can say, "You made a mistake. You, yourself, are good, valuable, and loved. You are worthy of better behavior. I am sure you can do it." The key is to maintain the integrity of the child's inherent value. The child's character is growing, and growth is a process. A child is a work in progress, and the essence of nurturing his growth is positive motivation.

So too with your marriage. Look back and evaluate how you used to deal with conflict and how you deal with it now. You are more mellow than you used to be. You have learned to differentiate between your spouse's person or self and his actions. If you want to stay married, then shut up about your spouse's character. Do not resort to putting him down as inconsiderate, lazy, or hurtful. Use "I" messages (see chapter 2) to comment on how you feel about the behavior of your spouse. "I was hurt when you said that," is much easier to deal with than "You" messages, like, "You are inconsiderate and selfish."

CHAPTER 23

and Eat Your Dinner

The most successful children are not the ones who come from the wealthiest homes or have the most extracurricular activities. They are not the ones who have the most educational toys or the most exciting vacations. According to a celebrated study by the National Center on Addiction and Substance Abuse at Columbia University, published in a report called "The Importance of Family Dinners",[3] the most successful children— that is to say—the most well-adjusted, balanced, self-sufficient and self-confident children—are the children who have dinner with their parents at least five evenings per week. Why?

When you have open communication with your children on a regular basis, when you sit with them eye to eye and actually listen to them and value their opinions, you give them a sense of inner security that you believe in them. They feel valued. This awareness enters their subconscious mind. Their sense of self is strengthened, and they gain a foundation of emotional security and support to take risks, to be willing to meet any challenge, and to strive to accomplish their goals.

Instead of giving them instructions, arguments, and lectures while you are standing and they are sitting or giving them last minute instructions as they are flying out the door, sit down and share thirty minutes of discussion with them over dinner. Then they get the sense that their parents have time for them and take them seriously. When you create consistent family time, not just occasional quality time, you are saying, "I have time for you because you are valuable to me, and your views and thoughts count in my eyes. Let's talk over dinner."

Finding time for our most important relationships is not easy. However, let's look at it this way: do we work to live or do we live to work?

I was in law school in Toronto and was coming home late from the library one night on the subway when I met an older friend who was already working as a lawyer. He was coming home late from work. He held up two briefcases and told me that he was even bringing work home from the office. "This briefcase is for Susie, and this briefcase is for Penny," he told me proudly. I said to myself, "His kids will be long asleep when he gets home, so he won't see them. And even if they were awake, he wouldn't have time to spend with them because he would be too busy with his take-home work. So what is the point of working for your children if you never see them?"

We work hard all our lives to provide for our children. We want to give them the things our parents were unable to provide for us. Does your child really need that new game, new pool table, or new baseball glove? Or has he been standing by the window with a ball in his hand, hoping that his father will have time to play catch with him? And will that game of catch ever come?

The same holds true with your spouse. You cannot be close to someone unless you spend time together. You need to spend quality time with your spouse every night to review the events of the day and discuss the plans for tomorrow and the rest of the week. Most people e-mail or text their spouses about the coordination of the day's events. Texting does not make for an emotional bonding. All it takes is fifteen minutes of direct face-to-face contact per day. Can you spare fifteen minutes for your spouse?

You might ask, "Why is that necessary? Why can't I just text my spouse about the technical arrangements of our lives? Bonding is necessary because married couples have nothing to say to each other after eight years, according to a research study. Professor Hans Jurgens asked five thousand German husbands and wives how often they talked to each other. After two years of marriage, most of them managed two or three minutes of chat over breakfast, more than twenty minutes over the evening meal, and a few more minutes in bed. By the sixth year, that total was down to 10 minutes a day. A state of "almost total speechlessness" was reached by the eighth year of marriage.[4]

We spend much more time with work colleagues, playing the weekly basketball game, in front of the television or on the computer than we do with our spouses. If marriage was a business arrangement, then you could text, make a conference call, and have monthly sales meetings. But marriage is a system for emotional support that can only happen face to face in real time, not just virtual time. It is not enough to try to squeeze in some free time to spend with your spouse. You have to make time for your relationship. When it comes to emotional support and spending quality time with your spouse, do not shut up. In this case you need to speak up and be there for your spouse.

CHAPTER 24 # SHUT UP

and Finish Your Unfinished Business

When we are children, we grow up in a particular family constellation based on our birth order. The eldest has her challenges. She has many responsibilities and is the guinea pig for her parents' anxieties. The middle child often suffers from the middle-child syndrome. Not being the star first-born and not being the baby of the family, the middle child often gets less attention and feels she must exert herself to get noticed. And the youngest gets all the privileges and is doted upon and has to learn to be assertive.

All children carry these issues into adulthood where they become "unfinished business" that must be sorted out when they get married. When spouses learn about each other's family upbringing they gain insight about their partners. They think, "Oh, that's why you are the way you are. I get it now."

The phenomenon of unfinished business—unresolved issues from childhood—is most prevalent in regard to low self-esteem. When parents are hypercritical, judgmental, and heavy disciplinarians, the result will often be a child with low self-esteem.

And this low self-image does not go away as the child grows into adulthood. When they marry and begin to create a family in their own home, their low self-esteem resurfaces and seriously affects the marriage.

A spouse with low self-esteem often mirrors the highly critical behavior that he saw growing up. He knows no other style other than the one he experienced growing up so he becomes critical of his own spouse. Or he becomes overly sensitive to innocuous comments and gets easily hurt or depressed or provokes an argument in response to a perceived insult.

The low self-esteem that pervades marriages is usually undiagnosed. The spouses fight, argue, and fall out of love. If they discover that the real issue is the unfinished business of low self-esteem that has been unresolved since childhood, then the low self-esteem can be addressed as we have discussed in this book. When the spouses improve their self esteem they can stop hurting each other by learning to shut up and stay married.

EPILOGUE

When you stop to think of how amazing it is to be alive—to see in color, to hear, to smell, taste, and touch the astonishing wonders of this world; to experience, with your senses, both the bitter and the sweet; to feel the contrasting emotions of sadness and happiness, lethargy and enthusiasm; to be able to transform your mood from despair to rhapsody with a mere attitude change and a shift in your way of thinking—the thought is truly awe-inspiring.

To be able to think negative and hurtful thoughts one second and then to take control of your mind and intellect and think thoughts of compassion the next is to transform yourself with the power of your own free will. To perform a hurtful act and then to be able to rectify it with a word of remorse and an act of kindness is to recreate yourself with your own inner strength.

To know the power of self-transformation by harnessing your inner Wheel of Strengths is to behold the awesome power that resides within your soul that allows you to take control of your own destiny. This is real power. It is an inner power, an inner strength of character. You can achieve a greatly elevated state, one with which you were born naturally, if only you appreciate the strengths that reside within your personality and activate them.

The family unit is the best laboratory within which to discover and share your best character traits. Your spouse is there for you to learn to use your compassion, patience, empathy, and sensitivity. Your children are there for you to realize that you are not the center of the universe and for you to become more humble and giving.

When your children face challenges at school or have social problems you need to identify with their pain and be emotionally present for them. When your spouse goes through a social crisis or a problem with his parents or siblings, you need to be supportive. This does not mean solving the problem for him. It means sharing the pain with him by telling him that you are with him in his pain and you will help him through it. This is using your character attributes and your true self to be emotionally supportive.

There are three basic components of the human psyche:
- The Physical Self: the body's instinctive knee-jerk responses
- The Emotional Self: the feeling self, where your emotions reside
- The Soul Self: the true self—the part of you which brings you intellectual, spiritual and creative fulfillment

We normally live in the middle level, the Emotional Self. We are happy, sad, motivated, depressed, and we need hugs. When someone hurts your feelings, your instinctive reaction is to move down to the Physical Self and respond in order to defend yourself. You might respond by insulting or hurting the other person in self-defense. Reacting instinctively is the autopilot response. Moving from your Emotional Self (being emotionally hurt) to your Physical Self (by lashing out in response), is natural. But that reaction would not be responding from your true self.

You'll find it much harder to go against gravity and rise above the Emotional Self and move into your Soul Self by using an 'I' message. Or you can access your Soul Self and respond with your best character traits and be emotionally supportive. That response would be reacting from your true self. That is what this book has set out to achieve—to give you the tools to recognize and to activate your true self. Since you may have been programmed with low self-esteem in childhood, you will need daily practice to get good at accessing your true self. But it can be done. You can do it. Use the tools and techniques you learned in this book and then you will be able to shut up, and you'll stay married.

NOTES

1. Fitts, William H., Tennessee Self Concept Scale, Western Psychological Services, 1965. The Wheel of Strengths is an adaptation of the Tennessee Self Concept Scale
2. Rogers, C.R., *Carl Rogers on Personal Power: Inner Strength and its Revolutionary Impact* (London: Constable, 1978).
3. "The Importance of Family Dinners," National Center on Addiction and Substance Abuse (CASA), Columbia University, 2005.
4. Felber, T., Am I Making Myself Clear, Nelson Thomas Inc., Nashville, 2002

ABOUT THE AUTHOR

Yisroel Roll, is an innovative psychotherapist, lawyer and skilled mediator with offices in Baltimore, Lakewood, and Toronto. A dynamic motivational speaker, he inspires audiences around the world with life-transforming marriage and parenting workshops. In Shut Up and Stay Married, his fifth book, he reveals a new approach to marriage success. He lives in Baltimore, Maryland with his wife and children.

Shut Up and Stay Married Workshops

Workshops are presented across the country in community centers, religious institutions, PTA gatherings and in-service training programs. The 90-minute interactive events are entertaining and provide practical, take-home strategies and tools. He also presents the Step Up to the Plate parenting and self esteem workshops. To schedule a workshop, contact Yisroel Roll at roll@shutupandstaymarried.com, www.shutupandstaymarried.com or call (410) 585-0497.

CPSIA information can be obtained at www.ICGtesting.com
231686LV00007B/27/P